One Small Step

How a Trans Am, a
Smashed Finger, and the
God of the Universe
Saved Our Family

Rick Rekedal

Special Thanks

Mickey Corcoran
For help with the cover art, thank you
for getting the highlights just right.

Christine Silk
For help with editing, thank you for your
gentle writer's coaching and guidance.

Vicki Rekedal
For reading drafts and patience with late-night
typing. Dad always says I married up.
He is 100% right.

Comments? Please email me at
rick.gossamertales@gmail.com

For the legacy to come:

Ingrid

Ellen

Eirene

Isabel

Audrey

Aaron

Dear Dad,

Whenever I tell you about someone I've met, you remind me that if it helps to tell them your story, I should feel free to do so. Over the years I have found it is impossible to tell my story without starting with yours.

There are many more who will be blessed to hear your story than I can tell in person. This is pretty much how I tell it. I fact-checked with Mom but didn't tell her why. In most ways this is Mom's story too, of course.

C.S. Lewis wrote about friendship in <u>The Four Loves</u>: "Friendship is born at that moment when one man says to another: 'What! You too? I thought that no one but myself...'" That is how I feel about you. I am proud to be your son.

Love,
Rick

The Silver Trans Am

I was seven years old when my dad came to pick me up for a weekend visit to his apartment in west Minneapolis, early in 1975. He was driving a Pontiac Trans Am. It was brand new, bright silver, with the classic screaming eagle on the hood. A few years later Burt Reynolds made the Trans Am the most popular car in the country in *Smokey and the Bandit*. But on that day, pulling into the driveway, Dad seemed like a stranger behind the wheel of that strange car.

My parents had been separated for a few months by then. Over the previous Christmas, my mom had taken my younger sister and me to Maryland to be with her side of the family. What we didn't know was that while we were gone, my dad moved out of our house. All I knew as we flew to Maryland was that spending Christmas vacation away from home without Dad gave me a new, empty feeling.

Dad stepped out of his new car and walked across our small lawn. I noticed his finger was black and flat. It looked ugly. He admitted he had slammed it in the door of his new car. My mom stifled a laugh.

She hated that car. I wasn't crazy about it, either, which was strange, because I loved cars. I had a big collection of Matchbox toys. My bed sheets turned into roads and driveways after I was tucked in for the night. I drove those cars under the covers and made up all sorts of little stories and scenarios, parking them under my pillow as I fell asleep. My two close friends were Peter Moe and John Fox. They both had Hot Wheels, while I was a purist with my Matchbox cars. But I don't remember being impressed with the Trans Am; I just felt confused and weird seeing Dad drive something that wasn't our family car.

He was there to take me away for the weekend. I had packed a little bag. He put me in the front seat, and the two of us, the men in my mom and little sister's life, pulled out of the driveway. We drove to his new apartment near Loring Park. I knew the area because in the winter we would ice skate on Loring Pond, but now I was going to stay at my dad's own, separate place. The upstairs apartment was yellowish inside, smelled like new vinyl chairs, with a small dimly lit kitchen.

It's funny the memories that stay with you. After 40 years I still remember how strange it felt to be in that apartment with my dad. He had an activity for us to do together: a Ronco glass cutter designed to cut off the tops of pop bottles and turn them into drinking glasses. We made two glasses out of green 7-Up bottles. Dad ran his flat blackened finger along the edges to make sure we wouldn't cut our lips.

Why am I writing about this? Several months ago I realized it's my job to record my dad's legacy. He needs to hear it and I need to tell it, both for my dad's sake and for the extended family and friends who are part of his legacy. It all started when my dad had the courage to take a step of asking for help in the midst of a crumbling marriage and alcoholism. This is the story of how we got to that point and what got us out. The day he took that step is the day our entire family began to change.

Chaos

The year before my dad moved out was marked with emotional chaos. Both my parents worked, so I was coming home after school to an empty house. My younger sister Robin must have been in daycare.

Alone on the walk home, sometimes I would wander around the neighborhood. Robert Fulton Elementary School was on Xerxes Ave and 50th St near Edina in south Minneapolis. Today it is called Lake Harriet Elementary. Heading home I would veer east a couple blocks toward Lake Harriet, or head west to Clancy's Drug Store where I could read comic books.

One day I felt particularly daring. I got on a city bus and took it all the way to Southdale mall. My friend Peter told me kids under ten could ride the city bus for free. Peter had a big brother, and his mom was a night nurse who slept at home during the day, which seemed exotic. Peter knew stuff, so I figured he was right about the bus. I stood at the bus stop on Xerxes Ave, looking up at the sign in the bus window that said "Southdale," the shopping center where we went as a family. Backpack and all, I climbed aboard, and sure enough the driver didn't ask me to pay. As a lone first grader I rode for two and a half miles to the mall and got out. I wandered a bit, then came back to the bus stop and caught the return bus back to my stop.

Usually, though, I would go home after school, let myself in the front door, pour a bowl of sugared cereal and switch on our black and white Motorola TV to watch Looney Tunes reruns. One afternoon,

Peter and John came over and we scooped huge bowls of ice cream, smothered in chocolate syrup. It was wonderful and guilt-inducing at the same time. Halfway through our afternoon sugar bath, we heard my mom's car pulling into the driveway earlier than expected. All-out group panic took over. Upstairs, the desk chair in my bedroom had a seat that opened like a piano-bench, a perfect place for hiding ice cream. We stacked our three bowls and squeezed the seat down on top of them. Peter and John quietly left for home. Mom found the mess, of course, melted and dripping onto my bedroom floor.

Amidst long periods of quiet tension, tempers flared. I remember running from my dad, out our back door and down the steps into the yard, frightened after he picked up a piece of wood and shook it at me. He had no intention of using it, but he was losing patience with a hyperactive kid.

Bedtime was a major stress point, always a long, drawn out affair. It was difficult for me to settle down and go to sleep. I slept fitfully and I was a bed wetter. Several nights a week I would pad down the hall to my parents' room, waking my mom to have my sheets changed. It got to the point where Mom would just lay down a towel for me to sleep on until morning.

Throughout 1974, deeper cracks were forming in my parents' marriage, but I never heard them fight. I have since read that most children of parents who separate are unaware their parents are unhappy. The kids usually don't see the separation coming. That's how it was with me. Only as an adult did I learn that a round of counseling in the fall of '74 didn't take. By December, Dad was done with the marriage and ready to leave, but Mom convinced him to stay through Christmas Eve.

As I mentioned before, on Christmas Day, my mom, Robin and I flew to Maryland without Dad, to see my mom's family near Washington D.C. Uncles and aunts surrounded us in Maryland, including my dad's brother who lived in Baltimore with his new wife. He remembers my mom as "shattered." Once again, I was unaware, but the grownups stayed up all night talking about what had gone wrong. By the time we returned to Minneapolis after the holidays, Dad had moved out of the house. He was gone.

I don't remember what he told us when we next saw him, but I remember at one point my mom came into my bedroom crying and said through her tears, "Your dad just said he's never coming back." I went back to playing on the floor. My mom tells me that sometime later I said, "Mom, don't worry, I'm going to do anything it takes to get Dad back."

On the surface I was fine. But my skinny, stressed little-boy self acted out in school, at home, and with friends. I had a few fights on the playground, including one that continued in my front yard after an older kid who punched me at school followed me home and punched me again. I covered up as many of those incidents as I could, never telling my parents.

I also fought with my mom. The two of us had a number of big battles. Once I convinced my younger sister Robin to dump her entire glass of milk out on the carpeted floor of our dining room. Sitting in her high chair, egged on by me, Robin poured the milk out just as Mom burst in from the kitchen. She was furious. She shouted and pointed, "Ricky, I heard you from the kitchen, you told her to do it!"

During one doozy of an argument I decided to run away. In a quiet rage, I hurriedly packed two pairs of underwear, socks, a transistor radio and the latest *Mad* magazine, stuffing everything into my school backpack. I was leaving Mom too, just like dad.

Feeling bold, I marched down the stairs and out the front door, heading to the corner of Xerxes and 47th Street. I looked back and saw Mom following me.

With mom on the hook I pressed on down the block. But looking back once more, I saw my mom turn around and walk back to our house.

I still remember the shock of realizing she wasn't coming after me. I had lost Dad, and now Mom was letting me go. My pace slowed. I finished walking the length of the block, then trudged home. I learned later Mom was acting on the understanding that calling my bluff and letting me "run away" proved I wouldn't get far before returning home. She was right. Mom was sitting quietly at the dining room table when I came inside. I walked up to her and we both broke down, crying in each other's arms. I couldn't leave Mom.

The house was pretty empty without Dad. In the end he was gone less than half a year, but his absence seemed permanent at the time. I experienced a lot of isolation and separation, with my mom working long hours and my sister in day care in the afternoons. I don't remember going to stay with my dad for other weekends except when we made the 7-Up bottle glasses.

But as lonely as things were for me, for my parents, the separation gave them time to realize they weren't ready to give up. Thankfully, my folks tried a second round of marriage counseling. This time, Dad realized the issue in their marriage wasn't my mom or us kids, but his lack of commitment and their poor communication skills. Once they recommitted to the marriage, they sought specific guidance on how to communicate better.

Their counselor was a Jewish therapist recommended by their Episcopalian minister. After five weeks of sessions and a follow-up a few months later, the therapist said they were doing great. They agreed, and decided to rededicate their marriage. Both my parents sang in the choir at St. Mark's Cathedral, an Episcopal church where my dad also had a gig as the paid baritone soloist. The dean of St. Mark's came to our house for the rededication service. Robin and I stood up with my parents, a little best man and maid of honor. There were about a dozen friends there. It was a joyful day.

A family united, we went to church on Easter. My parents took communion together for the first time in months. The priest, a friend of theirs, said he was so happy he didn't know whether to hug them or hit my dad over the head with the chalice.

I will always remember the day Dad moved back in. When Dad moved out, my mom noticed he had taken his pillow. Moving back in, his pillow was back on the bed, a memorable symbol on such a big day.

In the months following Dad's return, my folks worked on fitting their lives back together. But old friendships, habits and patterns were still part of the picture. The church choir at St. Mark's, long a social base for my folks, had also become a group of drinking buddies for my dad. After choir practice, Dad and a few friends had long parties into the night, and they knew how to drink. From week to week the pattern of drinking would develop into full-blown alcoholism. We didn't know it at the time, but we were about to face even more challenges as my dad's drinking deepened.

Father & Son

Today I am 47 years old with a family of my own, and my parents are a huge part of my life. I live in Los Angeles, travel all over the world for business, and have been married for 22 years to the woman of my dreams. We have three amazing, strong and beautiful daughters. My dad lives in Austin, Texas, with my mom, the same woman he walked out on in December 1974. They have a strong marriage, just a few years shy of their 50th anniversary. We don't see each other very often, but we talk on the phone almost every other day.

If I go a week without calling my dad I get antsy. We have a shorthand we've been using for years. I ask "Did I catch you at a good time?" and he says "I'm standing here at Home Depot trying to find the right size bolt," or "I'm sitting with your mom, say hi," as he puts me on speaker phone. Dad is deeply respected in his community. He is an elder in his church, a friend and mentor to pastors, professionals, missionaries, PhDs, millionaires, and neighbors across the street.

During worship in his church, if he sees someone weeping or in need, he leaves his seat and walks right over, stretching an arm of support around a shoulder, offering prayer or comfort. When I visit, he introduces me to people as his son he is so proud of, but they are all quick to tell me how much they love him. There are hundreds of people in the Austin area that have been deeply affected by my dad, and hundreds more whose lives he has touched.

The question is, what happened? What broke the patterns that created so much chaos in our young family? How did a man who left his wife and children, whose own church choir was part of his alcoholism, become a dedicated father and husband, a respected church elder and a mentor in the community?

The simple answer is this: My dad took a step – a step towards God. And God saved us.

It's true. It may sound trite or unintelligent. But I lived it, and still live it to this day. When Dad reached out, God showed up. He still shows up in our family today.

Robin and I have gone on to productive careers in vastly different fields. Robin and her husband Steve live and work overseas, dedicated to southern Asia. They have lived in their region for years, serving several hundred villages in their sphere of influence, reaching and touching the lives of thousands. They minister amidst a culture deeply rooted in several thousand years of caste system hegemony. They do an awesome, thankless work, marked by humble sacrifice and servant leadership. Robin and Steve live in the heart of perhaps the most crowded city in the world, dealing with the stress and challenges of raising three teenagers in a tiny flat. Amid such immersion they are a thriving, beautiful family.

I have worked in Hollywood and children's entertainment for over 25 years, and have been part of some of the biggest films in the business, but my name doesn't go above the title. I'm one of many behind-the-scenes executives who help shepherd projects out the door and into the culture. I love what I do and my work has introduced me to some incredibly powerful and famous people.

My wife Vicki and I have been blessed in so many ways. We still live in our first home, raising our girls to share one bedroom between the three of them, leaving the spare bedroom open for guests. Family friends, foreign missionaries, college buddies and grandparents have all stayed in our guest room over the years, including a young woman whose engagement broke off a month before her wedding and she needed a place to live.

We have tried to live within our means, choosing camping trips over cruises and paying off the credit card every month. I have a ton of flyer miles built up from business travel, so last November we flew my folks from Texas to join us on a family camping trip to Joshua Tree National Park. Dad hates to camp, Mom loves it. To ease the challenges of camping, we rented a large RV for them, while we used tents in the high desert.

The last day of our trip, Dad and I drove the RV back to LA while Vicki drove everyone else in our Toyota van. The drive allowed the two of us to talk the whole way back. We got to talking about a billionaire investor I had recently met, and I mentioned how the guy had set a few billion aside as a legacy for his foundation.

Then my dad said, "Well I don't have a legacy or anything like that, but it sure is great to see you and your sister doing so well." The conversation moved on but the wording of his remark stuck with me. *I don't have a legacy or anything like that.*

Of course we were talking about this billionaire and his private foundation, so I knew my dad meant he didn't have a billion dollars to leave to his grandkids, but he could have said "I'm not rich like that guy." Instead he said the words, "I don't have a legacy." That remark has stuck with me for months. So here's what I want to tell you about Steve Rekedal.

My dad has a tremendous legacy.

In many ways, his story began 40 years ago, in the basement of a building in west Minneapolis, not far from that lame apartment off Loring Park with the smell of vinyl chairs. On November 4, 1975, seven months after renewing his wedding vows, my 29-

year-old dad walked into an Alcoholics Anonymous (AA) meeting and said he needed help.

It was only the first step, but it was significant. Everything that was to follow started when he dared to take that one small step.

Church Choir Drinking Buddies

Dad entered the AA meeting and sat down. His drinking buddy of several years, who I'll call Dan, had invited him. Dan sang with my dad in the choir at St. Mark's. The two of them were a big part of keeping the drinking going at the after-practice parties.

Dad's bouts with alcohol had been part of his life since college and even before that. When he was 18, he was bailed out of the sheriff's office by his father in their small town of Howard Lake, Minnesota, having been picked up for public drinking.

Only two years later, my parents' marriage was launched in the distress of a tragic year in my dad's family. In January 1967, my dad's younger brother Brian took his own life in the basement of their family home just a few days before his 18th birthday. The shock of Brian's death gripped the family and the whole town. Within a matter of days Brian was buried in a quick funeral, and my dad returned to college, numb and ill equipped to process his brother's suicide.

Understandably, in the midst of such turmoil, my folks turned to each other. By spring of that year, at age 20 and 21, Dad and Mom were married. The wedding was put together so quickly my mom's parents didn't attend. They were living in Africa and couldn't travel to Minnesota in time. Mom's older brother David walked her down the aisle instead of her father. That weekend, the young newlyweds had a quick two-day honeymoon. Stopping at a liquor store, my dad sent his new wife in to buy the booze, since she had already turned 21 and my dad was still only 20. They were back at school within a week of getting married. By the end of that year, I was born. I am named Richard Brian in memory of my uncle Brian, born in December of the year he died. On the anniversary of Brian's death at the end of January 1968, I was already five weeks old. In one brief year, my dad had lost a brother, gained a wife, and fathered a son.

Things stayed intense from there. My parents suffered a miscarriage two years later. To this day my mom says the first person she wants to meet in heaven is the son she never knew from that miscarriage. My sister Robin was born two years after that, followed by the purchase of their first house in Minneapolis. Dad's drinking increased. We have home movies of my two-year-old sister taking an empty beer bottle down from the picnic table and simulating drinking out of it, grownups laughing in the background. Our pet parakeet would fly around the house, tame and friendly, and land on the rim of someone's glass, learning to sip the sweet alcohol. This lasted until he died on the floor of his cage, passed out drunk. Things are pretty bad when the family parakeet dies of delirium tremens.

Over the next few years Dad's drinking intensified. By his mid-twenties it was usually masked in the social overlay of church choir parties, Dad and Dan staying to the end. While my parents were separated and then got back together in 1975, Dad had not seen Dan for some time. However, one day Dan called my dad up and said he had stopped drinking. That was a shock. Dan described his experience of going to an AA meeting, and invited my dad to come with him. I don't know if my dad struggled with the idea, but as he considered Dan's invitation, eventually it landed. Dad called Dan and said he would go to a meeting to check it out.

They're Telling My Story

Sitting in a smoke-filled church basement on a cold November night in 1975, my dad listened to the AA guys tell their stories. As they talked, he heard his own story told by three different people. For the first time, Dad felt he wasn't alone in his struggles with alcohol. By the end of the meeting he realized he needed to give it up...but just for today.

His entire life changed at that moment. My dad is quick to say he never thought about giving up drinking for the rest of his life; rather, he asked God for just enough strength to get through the rest of that day. Those days have come one day at a time for over 39 years. Ever since then, my dad celebrates his "sober birthday" on November 4, marking the day since 1975 when he gave up drinking.

Miraculously, Dan had gone from being my dad's drinking buddy to his AA sponsor. A sponsor is a person who has made some progress in recovery from alcoholism, and shares that experience with someone who is attempting or maintaining sobriety. The sponsor is actively involved in the life of the person they are sponsoring, providing support and accountability on a consistent basis. The bottom line is, you can't do it alone.

As of November 4, 2015, it will be 40 years. To this day my dad has stayed sober. He has not had a drink except for two instances. One is that if he is in a church that serves wine for communion, he will take dip the bread and taste a little of the wine in his communion.

The other happened once, many years later, when he was at an NBA game and discovered non-alcoholic beer. Dad loved the taste of beer in his drinking days, and learning about the invention of non-alcoholic beer was a revelation. He ordered one and it tasted amazing, having not had a cold beer for so many years. But halfway through the bottle he felt a slight buzz coming on. He looked closely at the label: "Contains 0.5% alcohol." His sober system felt the effect like a shot. He threw the bottle away, not finishing the contents. That was it.

Lifelong Sponsorship

My dad's current AA sponsor is in his 80s, an amazing man of strong faith and conviction who himself has been sober for 44 years. I had the privilege of meeting him recently when my dad introduced us over a Frosty at a local Wendy's.

My dad's sponsor showed me the 44-year chip he carries in his pocket every day, plus a 24-hour chip he also carries. A chip is a round coin-style token about the size of a half-dollar, marking how many days, months or years a person has remained sober. The 24-hour chip is the first token an AA member is given when they take their initial step toward sobriety.

When my dad's sponsor has trouble thinking about lasting 44 years, he simply turns to the 24-hour chip, asking God for the strength to get through today without a drink. Dad also carries two chips, one for 24 hours and one for 39 years. The 39-year chip belonged to his sponsor, who passed it to my dad, creating a unique bond of friendship between them. After talking with both of them, I got the impression that the 24-hour chip is more relevant. Every day is another opportunity to stay sober, one day at a time.

When Dad took his first step with AA, he had been through deep family tragedy and marital struggles throughout his 20's. Yet somehow he found the strength, humility and honesty to admit he needed help. As it turned out, however, that first step paved the way for an even bigger step to follow.

Up to that point in our family life, going to church was an expected part of our family culture, but was not always a deep source of spiritual guidance or comfort. My dad's parents had stoically put away thoughts of their son's suicide, burying hurt and grief that would surface decades later when they celebrated their 50th anniversary. Their dedication and involvement in the Lutheran church was a given, but at the time their broader family influence over us didn't instill a deeper understanding of the Bible nor an active daily faith.

By now my dad was in the early days of AA, led to sobriety initially by his former church choir drinking buddy. But AA had done something more. AA introduced my dad to a new concept of God. There is a higher power in the universe, a power we can choose to call God, a source of strength to make it through each day. With this new understanding of God, along with the support of a trusted sponsor, working the twelve steps of AA, and pursuing community with fellow AA members, my dad found sobriety possible.

AA's call to believe in God has been adopted and embraced by agnostics, atheists, people of nominal faith, of any background, for one simple reason: AA encourages you to simply believe in the God you understand. Not a denomination or an organized church, or any formal religion or set of Bible verses, but simply the God you know.

This appeal to the help of a higher power, to the concept of God a person already has, was an easier step for my dad to take. It helped get his eyes off himself and onto something, or Someone, he could call on in moments of need. And it worked, just as it has worked for thousands of recovered alcoholics helped through AA.

As my dad began walking daily in his sobriety, the Serenity Prayer made famous by AA soon went up on our wall, and remained framed in our house for years: "God grant me the serenity to accept the things I cannot change, the courage to change the things I can, and the wisdom to know the difference." I like to swap "serenity" for "grace" when I say the prayer myself.

But Dad's sobriety uncovered a stark reality. Even though their marriage was back together, the drinking had masked a deeper need for stability between my parents. Once the alcohol was removed, there was nothing to hide the enormity of the challenges they faced in trying to hold their marriage together. Our family needed a more solid foundation. Little did they know it would come from a surprising place. The next big step was upon them.

Faith

An AA friend, aware of the fragility of their lives, recommended the two of them try a neighborhood Bible series called the Faith Study, led by a local pastor named John Eagan. John went on to lead a large church in the Minneapolis area, only to resign in 2002 following a sad infidelity scandal. But in 1977 my parents attended the Faith Study that John led in the neighborhood. This didn't seem like a big stretch at the time. They justified they had been raised in the church, and AA had sparked a new understanding of God in my dad.

Yet it didn't take long before that Bible study began to change their lives. The Faith Study laid out a simple explanation of God's love in a way they had never heard before. Although each of them had been raised in church-going families, the idea that Jesus was who he said he was, and was interested in a uniquely personal relationship with them, was new. After everything they had been through, the gospel message they heard was intimate and real.

Within a few weeks, but independently of each other, my parents came to a new understanding of God's love. They became Christians. More time passed before they would gather the courage to admit what they had done, neither realizing the other had become a Christian.

Today the word "Christian" is loaded with baggage, so here is some context for how it came to be. The term was first used about 2,000 years ago by the Roman Empire, which needed a label for the followers of Jesus Christ. The Romans thought they were rid of Jesus when they executed him, but in the years after his crucifixion (and claimed resurrection), the small band of disciples he left behind quickly grew to tens of thousands of followers. Roman soldiers derisively called them "Christ-ians," or little Christs, ridiculing them for their piety. Christians wore the term as a badge of honor.

Roman culture was deeply stratified by class and race. Perpetual slavery, gladiatorial blood sport and the killing of baby daughters by exposure were accepted practices. By contrast the Christians of Rome practiced unconditional acceptance and equality. They modeled the example and encouragement of the apostle Paul, imprisoned in Rome but allowed to teach among them for at least two years during the early days of the church. Christians endured persecution, welcomed the unwanted and became known by their love. Generation by generation their reputation grew.

Within a few hundred years, something happened which would have been unimaginable to the early converts from the time of Jesus. Christianity became the official religion of the entire Roman Empire. Historian Will Durant, in *The Story of Civilization*, remarks on "the sight of the Christians, scorned and oppressed by a succession of emperors, bearing all trials with a fierce tenacity, multiplying quietly, building order while their enemies generated chaos, fighting the sword with the word, brutality with hope, and at last defeating the strongest state that history has ever known."

However, this new status brought problems as well. Emperor Constantine made the church official but used it to justify political maneuverings. Centuries later, European states launched the regrettable Crusades, invoking their beliefs to justify destructive acts of war against Muslim nations, stoking unrest that still reverberates today. In his seminal book, *The Jesus I Never Knew*, Philip Yancey says: "Problems seem to arise when the church becomes too external, and gets too cozy with government."

Yet, the core tenets of the Christian faith endure. From Mother Theresa to Martin Luther King Jr., from AIDS hospices in Africa to house churches in communist China, Christians continue to live out the example of grace, compassion and acceptance modeled by Jesus, touching the hearts of millions.

For our little Minnesota family in the 1970s, the Faith Study marked a new beginning. We went through an almost immediate conversion experience when my parents became Christians. Our house felt like a whole new home. Robin and I settled down into a new security. Dad and Mom were loving and pleasant around each other. When they argued it didn't end with anyone walking away; they worked it out. I wasn't coming home to an empty house after school. My mom had to buy me husky-size jeans as I calmed down and filled out. My dad gave us a present, *The Children's Big Book of Bible Stories*. Filled with illustrations of battles, shepherds, camels and deserts, I spent hours poring over those pages.

One night the four of us sat together on the couch as Dad read us a story out of that book. I looked up and saw my dad crying. Tears ran down his face. I stared at him until he looked at me. Breaking into a smile, he said simply, "Nothing is wrong. I'm just so happy." From restoring their marriage to entering sobriety to becoming Christians, everything had completely changed for our little family in just a few short years.

A New Family

One night later that month, my dad knelt next to my bed as he tucked me in. He explained that our family had been restored because of God's love for us. He asked me if I wanted that same love to be with me for the rest of my life. In a moment that is still crystal clear to me I said, "Yes, Daddy, I would like Jesus in my heart."

That night, my dad, who had once told my mom he was never coming back, led me in the classic salvation prayer that has been prayed by millions of Christians. I was nine years old. My mom sat with my sister Robin as she did the same.

Dad re-committed himself as the breadwinner of our family, and his career in the insurance industry began to take off. Soon he took a new job in Virginia as marketing director and we moved away from Minneapolis for good, leaving behind the St. Mark's drinking buddies and the house with memories of my parents' separation. In the years to follow, we would move to the country of Panama, then out to southern

California, where I finished high school and enrolled in Biola University.

I attended Biola, a Christian college, without hesitation. Yet it was there that my faith unraveled. Out on my own, my doubts about the logic of God and whether the Bible is true overshadowed the faith of my childhood. My belief in God wavered until a worship service when I was 23 years old re-introduced me to the God that had saved my family. I discovered a simpler sense of who God was, and that I could turn to him for help. It was my own version of the AA appeal, learning to accept the God I knew, not someone else's version. Since then I have had a lifelong walk of moving from the God I understand to the God who is. I have many struggles and doubts, but the one thing I always come back to is that God saved my family. Of that I have no doubt.

Grieving Released

On July 10, 1993, Vicki and I were married in California, and the whole extended family was there. Six weeks later, my dad's side of the family reunited in Arkansas for his parents' 50th anniversary. During the reunion, my grandmother Ruth pulled me aside. "I have something for you," she said, producing a cardboard box. She spoke plainly, like a rehearsed speech. "These are your uncle Brian's things. I haven't touched them since the week he died. I am giving them to you. You can do with them whatever you wish. Throw them away or keep them for yourself, but I am ready to let them go."

Grandma Ruth was calm and steady. I sat there for a moment and digested what was happening. Opening the box, I found Brian's glasses, his Boy Scout hat, some school papers, other keepsakes. These were his personal effects, a time capsule preserved from the week he died. Taking her word that this unexpected treasure was freely mine, it only took me a moment to quietly decide what to do. I thanked her solemnly and assured her I would take care of it. Grandma Ruth left the room. She never mentioned it again.

That afternoon I asked my parents, uncles and aunts, their spouses, and my sister Robin if they would meet with Vicki and me after the younger cousins had gone to bed. Øystein Bjørdal, our great family friend from Norway, also joined us. Gathering in a bedroom, I told how Grandma Ruth had presented me with a box of family heirlooms earlier that day, and gave express permission to do with it whatever I wished. I placed the box in the middle of the room and said, "So I am giving it to you."

I watched as my dad, his brother and sister opened the box and began to remove Brian's things. The room fell silent. After a few moments, tears began to flow. They gently held those items, passing them to each other, the physical contact and recognition opening up memories long-since closed. Grieving and loss that had been buried with Brian since 1967 poured out that night.

Øystein's presence was a double blessing; he had come into the family in the years just after Brian's death, and was treated like a son by my grandparents. He was also a pastor, and served the family as such that night. His gentle touch and warmth helped usher in a healing sense of grace and compassion that now reached into the next generation.

We sat up until well past midnight, sharing a family experience of grief overdue by 25 years. Since then, when I am in Minneapolis traveling on business, I sometimes rent a car and drive out to Howard Lake to place flowers on Brian's grave. What was a long drive when I was kid now takes less than an hour, a brief pilgrimage to honor Brian's memory and acknowledge that what brought such great tragedy into the family has found a place of healing.

A Richer Legacy

I am grateful that my wife Vicki is committed to her faith. Her strong character is shaped in large part by her dad and mom. Steady and faithful, Vicki's father is an anchor for his family with a strong legacy of his own. When I married his only daughter he welcomed me into the family and has become a good friend and mentor. In our community Vicki is admired by many new moms seeking her counsel, support and advice. She has served as a doula for several births among close friends.

We have opened our home to younger couples in our community, and enjoy a broad network of dozens of families and hundreds of friends throughout southern California and across the country. We are invested in mission work in Asia, Africa, and the former Soviet Union. My work in Hollywood has made me part of projects that have reached literally millions around the world, and opened up doors on the speaking circuit. It is exciting and a little scary to travel around the world and meet so many people who say they have been inspired by work I was a small part of.

All of this impact stems back to that November night in 1975, when my dad took a courageous step of simple faith and asked God to help him stop drinking. If my dad had never taken that step, had never humbled himself and admitted he needed help, none of the above would have unfolded. The family healing wouldn't have happened the way it did, and none of the lives that my parents have affected would have had the chance to hear and see God's love through their friendship and ministry.

My dad is a hero for taking that step. I know he doesn't see it that way at all. He sees it as a moment of utter honesty and desperation. He looks at his finger, still scarred after all these years from the silver Trans Am, and remembers the blind hubris of buying that stupid car. He's right, of course. But only partially. It was a brave, heroic moment.

In owning his actions and admitting his condition, in many ways my dad became a man that day. However, it was only the first step. AA's twelve steps are hard work. Many who begin AA lack commitment or the humility to get through all the steps and live in healthy recovery. The steps include making a list of those you have wronged; going to each of them and asking forgiveness; making restitution to any you harmed or robbed; and reaching out and helping others through recovery.

Once he raised his hand, Dad committed himself to the humbling work of submitting to the twelve steps, all while learning to ask God for help and continuing to self-identify as an alcoholic.

Today my parents live in Texas, where they have been for the last 20 years. Wherever they go my parents have quickly built deep, trusting, life-long friendships. They have counseled dozens of couples in their marriages and matters of faith. In his travels my dad has found AA communities all over the world, and still goes to weekly meetings. He sponsors AA members and has a sponsor himself.

Dad has the ability to reach out in a way that wins trust. When he extends his hand, people sense there is real wisdom in this man. He spends long hours studying and reading the Bible and books by favorite authors C.S. Lewis, Watchman Nee and Oswald Chambers. He prays hard and consistently, for people he meets, his wife, his grandchildren, for Robin and me and our spouses.

Legacy

I came around on the Trans Am. Wisely, Dad didn't keep the car. But a couple years later I fell head over heels for Burt Reynolds' black Trans Am – it was even cooler than a Corvette. A restored version with the cheesy screaming eagle on the hood still turns my head. As a young boy, that weekend trip to my dad's apartment was a journey I never thought I would have to make. But years later we took another trip, this time with me in the driver's seat, my sober dad wondering about his legacy. I will never forget it. I promised myself I would tell his story. The first small deliberate step he took in 1975 began a new journey that reaches far beyond my sister and me, to the generational healing of our family, the hundreds Dad and Mom have reached directly, and the thousands more those people have reached.

Yet there is more to come. My parents have six grandchildren, all of whom strongly identify with the faith of their grandpa and grandma. They are steeped in Christian tradition, yet also hungry for what God is doing new today. As they meet and marry their spouses, their new young families will be living out the faith of their grandparents and parents. The legacy continues.

Dad, thank you for having the courage and humility to take that first step. Looking back, it was the biggest step of all.

Postscript: A Response To My Son, Rick

Your mom and I were born in 1946, the earliest of the Baby Boomer generation following WWII. By the time we were in college in the 1960s, our generation was in full pursuit of a social revolution through dropping "in" (drugs and alcohol) and dropping "out": college riots, Woodstock, Vietnam war protests, relaxed attitudes toward divorce, and much more. We had many excuses and conjured up many motivations to escape from reality.

My particular alcoholism, however, was not caused by any of these social influences, nor by the family and traditions in which I was raised. Many compare the effect of drinking to an allergy, provoking a chemical or biological change after even one drink. A key element in my recovery through the Twelve Step program of Alcoholics Anonymous is to own my behavior and take responsibility for the chaos that my drinking caused. I have learned to accept a fundamental concept that my sponsors and the program have taught, until it is now embedded in me: "One drink is too many—a thousand are not enough."

As you have so accurately presented, quality sobriety and progressive serenity happens in community where AA's Twelve Steps are practiced. This experience inevitably led me to a spiritual awakening to the "God of my understanding."

You have lovingly pronounced my legacy. Without hesitation, I humbly embrace the blessing of your words, and your passion to tell this part of our family's story, which we now know is really a small part of His story.

I've heard it said, "When you see the son you also see the father." How proud I am that you are my son, and that our Father God has shown me how to be your dad. Thank you, my dear son.

Recommended Reading

The classic blue-covered book <u>Alcoholics Anonymous</u> and its companion <u>Twelve Steps and Twelve Traditions</u> can be found at any bookseller, as well as the website <u>www.aa.org</u>, which offers information on how to find free AA meetings in your neighborhood.

Al-anon and Alateen (<u>www.al-anon.org</u>) have helpful information if you have been affected by someone else's problem drinking.

Judith S. Wallerstein's groundbreaking book <u>The Unexpected Legacy of Divorce</u> (Hachette) provides a startling picture of the surprisingly negative effects of divorce on children, reporting on the "divorce generation" that began in the 1970s. Wallerstein's book is a valuable resource for anyone contemplating divorce where children are involved.

BACK COVER

This small book tells the true, intimate story of our Midwestern American family in the 1970s, facing the challenges of alcoholism and separation in a young marriage. Mostly it's the story of my dad and how much I love and admire him.

Made in the USA
Middletown, DE
25 August 2024

59167300R00028